CANADIAN INVENTORS

To the memory of Mike Pastorius,
a proud Canadian and an inventor in his own right.
– M.T.

Photo Credits

Page 2, 4, 6 (lower), 8 (left and right), 9 (right),10 (upper and lower): Library of Congress, Prints and Photographs Division PPMSC 02854; PPMSC 00833; PPMSC 00837; LC-G9-Z1-144,963-A; LC-G9-Z1-156,508-A; LC-D420-2586; PPMSC 00897; PPMSC 00899

Page 3: R. Moffatt Studio, Portrait of Alexander Graham Bell, ca. 1914-1919, National Archives of Canada C-017335

Page 5, 9 (left): Alexander Graham Bell Family Papers, Manuscript Division, Library of Congress

Page 6 (upper): National Archives of Canada PA-030824

Page 7, 11, 21 (upper): Courtesy of A&T Archives via SODA; Ken Karp via SODA; Richard Hutchings via SODA

Page 12, 13, 14, 15, 16, 17: The Dr. James Naismith Basketball Foundation

Page 19: Glenbow Archives NA-3521-3

Page 20: Courtesy of the Canadian Wheelchair Basketball Association

Page 21 (lower): Naismith Memorial Basketball Hall of Fame

Page 22, 23, 25, 26, 27, 28, 29, 30, 31: J. Armand Bombardier Museum

Page 24: Sherbrooke Seminary Archives SPB101.001

Page 32, 33, 34 (upper), 36, 37, 38, 39: Courtesy of the Zimmerman family

Page 34: David F. Gray, University of Western Ontario

Page 40: CP/Rick Koza

Page 41, 44, 45: Courtesy of Research In Motion (RIM)

Page 43: Courtesy of UW Graphics

Page 46 (left): Bruce Hawkins

Page 46 (right): Courtesy of The Ernest C. Manning Awards Foundation

The author would like to thank Brian Wood, curator of The Bell Homestead National Historic Site; Gunner Laatunen for his assistance with the details of James Naismith's life; Guy Pépin for his help with Joseph-Armand Bombardier; and the Zimmerman family.

National Library of Canada Cataloguing in Publication

Trottier, Maxine
Canadian inventors / Maxine Trottier.

(Scholastic Canada biographies)
ISBN 0-439-96970-0

1. Inventors—Canada—Biography—Juvenile literature. 2. Inventions—Canada—History—Juvenile literature. I. Title. II. Series.

T39.T76 2004   j609.2'271   C2003-904906-X

6 5 4 3 2 1   Printed in Canada   04 05 06 07 08

Scholastic Canada Biographies

CANADIAN INVENTORS

Maxine Trottier

cover illustration by
Jock McRae

Scholastic Canada Ltd.
Toronto New York London Auckland Sydney
Mexico City New Delhi Hong Kong Buenos Aires

Alexander Graham Bell at the opening of the long distance line in Chicago

Alexander Graham Bell
The Inventor of the Telephone

From the day he was born, Alexander Bell's life was one of silence and sound. His mother was hearing-impaired. Both his father and grandfather worked in the study of speech. These facts set the course of his entire life and prepared him for the great things he would do. "Before anything else," he would later say, "preparation is the key to success."

Aleck, as he was called at home, came into the world on March 3, 1847, in Edinburgh, Scotland. He was the second boy in a family of three brothers. At age 11, he chose "Graham" – the name of a family

Aleck "Graham" Bell at the age of 11

friend – as his middle name, to set him apart from his grandfather and father, who were also called Alexander.

Like his brothers, Aleck was home-schooled, although he did spend one year in a private school and two years in Edinburgh's Royal High School, from which he graduated when he was 14. The next year he went to London, England, to work with his grandfather, a famous speech teacher. There he studied both electricity and sound. He experimented with massaging his dog's vocal cords and mouth so that when it whined it sounded like, "How are you, Grandmamma?"

By age 16, Aleck was teaching music and speech at a boys' boarding school. When he was 17, his father developed something he called Visible Speech, a system of symbols to describe sounds and how the tongue, lips and throat should be positioned to speak. It helped people who were speech- and hearing-impaired.

Because Aleck's father was so famous, there were often visitors from other countries in the Bell house, speaking different languages. Aleck and his brother would amaze them with the effectiveness of Visible Speech. One would write down the sounds of the visitor's language as symbols. Then the other would "read" them, perfectly pronouncing the words of a language he didn't know.

Aleck attended the University of Edinburgh, and continued to teach and experiment. Then, within three years of each other, both of Aleck's brothers died of tuberculosis, a disease of the lungs.

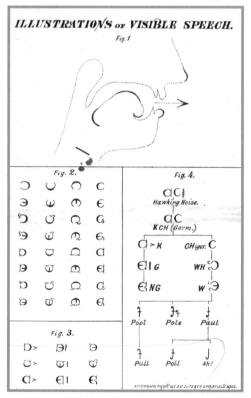

Visible Speech chart

Heartbroken, but determined to find a healthier climate for their remaining son, the Bells emigrated to Canada in 1870. Once here, they moved into a large farmhouse near Brantford, Ontario. All his life Aleck would refer to Melville House – as their home was called – as his "dreaming place."

In 1871 Alexander Graham Bell moved to the United States and opened his own school for the hearing-impaired. Two years later he became a professor of speech at the University of Boston. One

Melville House

Bell (upper right) at the Pemberton Avenue School
for the Deaf, Boston, 1871

Helen Keller at age 21 with Alexander Graham Bell

of his students was six-year-old Helen Keller. Another was 17-year-old Mabel Hubbard. He fell in love with her, and eventually they became engaged. When they were married in 1877, Aleck gave his bride all but 10 of his shares in the newly formed Bell Telephone Company as a wedding gift.

Bell had begun experimenting with electricity as a means of transmitting sound. Using a stalk of hay and the ear of a dead man, he saw that when he spoke into the ear, the stalk vibrated and traced the sound waves on a piece of smoked glass. He felt sure that sound waves could be carried by electrical wires.

Portraits of Alexander Graham and Mabel

In the summer of 1874, while visiting his parents at their home in Brantford, Bell got the idea for the telephone. He continued to work on his invention for many months. On March 10, 1876, at his Boston home, he spoke into the telephone he had created. "Mr. Watson," he said to his assistant, who was listening in another room. "Come here. I want to see you." The first telephone call had been made.

Back in Canada five months later, the first long-distance call was made between the telegraph office in Paris, Ontario, and Brantford, 13 kilometres away. On August 10, 1876, Bell heard his Uncle David say, "To be or not to be . . ." over the wires.

Four years later France awarded Alexander

Graham Bell a prize for inventing the telephone. He used the money to open a lab in Washington, DC. By this time he had two young daughters, and was a wealthy man, free to work on his other inventions.

Although he became a U.S. citizen in 1882, for the rest of his life he and his family returned every summer to their home at Baddeck on Cape Breton Island, Nova Scotia. Sometimes there for as long as six months, Bell worked on models of helicopters, and enormous kites on which a person could ride. Among other things, he invented the audiometer,

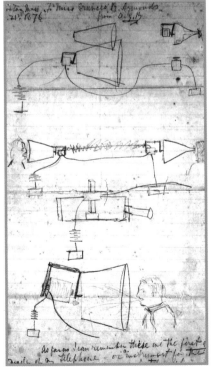

Bell's notebook sketch of a telephone

A model of Bell's first telephone, the instrument used to make the first phone call in 1875

Bell with the *Cygnet* on Baddeck Bay, 1907. This tetrahedral kite flew for seven minutes, lifting a man higher than 50 metres into the air.

which tested hearing, and a system of air conditioning. In 1909 an airplane that he and four others invented, the *Silver Dart*, was the first to fly in Canada.

Alexander Graham and Mabel watch the flight of the *Silver Dart* from a sleigh on the frozen bay.

Alexander Graham Bell never became a Canadian citizen, but his ties to this country remained close, and so we have come to consider him one of our own. He died at his Baddeck home on August 2, 1922. During his funeral service, every telephone in the entire Bell system was silenced for one minute, to honour the man who found such a wonderful way for people to communicate.

1960s Bell telephone

James Naismith
The Inventor of Basketball

James Naismith was born on November 6, 1861 in Almonte, Ontario. In 1869 he moved with his family to Grand Calumet, Ontario, where his father worked as a sawhand. When he was nine years old, both his parents died of typhoid fever. Orphaned, James, his brother Robbie and his sister Annie spent the next two years living in Bennie's Corners with their grandmother. When she died in 1873, the children were taken in by their Uncle Peter, who was a very strict man.

    James had chores to do before school, and so he

learned to work alone in the woods and drive a team of horses. Not the best student in the class, his talents lay elsewhere. He was a leader among his classmates in physical activities.

Life was not all work and studying. Children gathered at the blacksmith's shop at Bennie's Corners. James and his friends played in the woods. He learned to hunt with a bow and arrow. In winter, there was tobogganing and hockey. James made himself a pair of skates by fastening iron files onto pieces of wood.

After high school, James went on to study at McGill University in Montreal. To stay fit, he worked out in the university gymnasium and played

James "Jim" Naismith and a friend

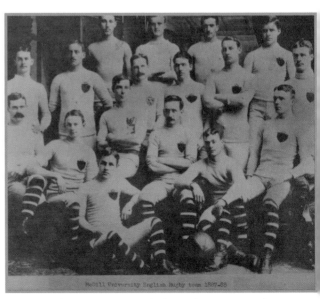

McGill University English Rugby Team, 1887-1888

Naismith (second from right) with fellow students on the editorial staff of the *Presbyterian College Journal* at McGill University

sports. In 1887, he graduated as one of the top ten in his class. Hard work had paid off.

James decided to continue his studies, so he enrolled in theological school to study religion. He won scholarships, but to make ends meet he worked as an instructor in the McGill gymnasium.

Once during a rugby game, another player swore in front of James. The man apologized to him, saying, "I didn't notice you were there." This incident gave James the idea that perhaps he could influence young people for the better through sports. He graduated from Presbyterian College, but decided to pursue a career in athletics and teaching.

In the summer of 1890, James Naismith enrolled at the YMCA training school in

The YMCA gym in Springfield, Massachusetts

Springfield, Massachusetts. He came to realize that there was a gap in the sports program. Between the end of football season and the beginning of baseball in the spring, there were only indoor activities in the gym. Students weren't happy with the situation and some began to drop out. What was needed was an indoor game that would keep the students physically fit as well as interested. In 1891 Naismith was assigned the task of inventing a new game.

He looked back to his childhood. There was a game they had played called "Duck on the Rock." They would place a stone on a large rock and take turns throwing stones to knock it off. It took skill, not brute force. Naismith decided that skill would be essential to the new game he now had in mind.

He sorted out all his ideas about the game, finally typing out 13 points. These would be the game's rules. Then, taking a soccer ball, he went to the gym where he ran into Pop Stebbins, the custodian. When James Naismith asked Pop if he had a couple of boxes, Pop said, "No, but I have a couple of peach baskets."

Naismith posted the 13 rules on the bulletin board. He nailed the peach baskets to a running track that circled the gym 10 feet above the floor. Then he called down his class of 18 men and, as two teams, they spent the class tossing the ball as they

Game and equipment as used in 1892

ran up and down the court. Later Naismith would say, "The class took to it, and the only difficulty I had was to drive them out when the hour ended."

It was December 21, 1891. James Naismith had invented "basket ball." There was another school nearby, and the students and teachers began coming to watch the games. Eventually, the girls asked if they could play and Naismith agreed. Soon the girls had a team of their own, playing in the long skirts that they wore at that time. By 1893 players were using baskets that were made of iron hoops and a hammock of netting. Ten years later the open-ended net was in use.

In 1898 Naismith went to the University of Kansas to work as the Director of Physical Education and as Chapel Director. He was the head coach for the first official basketball game held there on February 3, 1899. Naismith continued to serve the university and his community for 39 years — as a coach, a minister and a medical doctor. He had the opportunity to attend the 1936 Olympics in Berlin, Germany, and watch the first Olympic basketball game. "Doc" Naismith retired the next year at the age of 76.

During those years he had seen basketball grow in popularity. One Canadian team, the "Grads," or the Edmonton Commercial Graduates, were the champions of the game from 1915-1940. These women won 502 out of the 522 games that they played all over the world. Naismith said, "They are the finest team that ever stepped out on a floor."

James Naismith was inducted into Springfield's Basketball Hall of Fame in its first year, 1959. In 1978 he was the first inductee into the Canadian Basketball Hall of Fame in Almonte. Today, the game he invented is played in school gyms, on public courts and in suburban driveways. It is an Olympic

The Edmonton Commercial Graduates Basketball Club, 1924.
This team went to the Olympics in Paris, France.

sport, a wheelchair sport, and a professional sport, packing stadiums with thousands of cheering fans. Now played in over 170 countries, it is one of the most popular games in the world. James Naismith, though, saw it in simple terms. As he once said, "Basketball is just a game to play . . . You just play it."

Naismith·Memorial Basketball Hall of Fame, Springfield, Massachusetts

Joseph-Armand as a boy, in 1916 and in 1921;
a model of the toy train engine he made in 1920;
his home and family (ca. 1910)

Joseph-Armand Bombardier
The Inventor of the Snowmobile

When André Bombardier arrived in Quebec around 1700, he was faced with winters unlike those he had known back in France. A soldier, his determination earned him the nickname "Passe-Partout," or "Nothing Stands in His Way." More than 200 years later, that nickname would suit one of his descendants perfectly.

That person, Joseph-Armand Bombardier, was born the eldest of eight children in Valcourt, Quebec, on April 16, 1907. From the very beginning he was interested in mechanics. At the age of 13 he built one of his first mechanical toys, a small train engine driven by a clock mechanism. He needed money to buy some of the parts from the village jeweller, so he used what he was paid for serving Mass at the church. It was the start of many such creations.

To keep him from tinkering with the engine of his own car, Joseph-Armand's father gave him an old Model T Ford, one that was beyond repair. With the help of his brother Léopold, he had it running in short order.

Hoping their son would join the priesthood, Joseph-Armand's parents sent him to study at the

Saint-Charles-Borromée Seminary, Sherbrooke, Quebec

The strange looking sled, 1922

Saint-Charles-Borromée Seminary in Sherbrooke when he was 14. But his passion continued to be mechanics. Now he dreamed of building a machine that could be used for winter travel, something that could move over the snow. In places where people were so isolated by severe winter weather, it could be very important.

On New Year's Day, when he was home for the Christmas holidays, Joseph-Armand astonished his family when he and his brother pulled a strange looking sled out of his father's workshop. Joseph-Armand started up the Model T motor that propelled it and Léopold steered with the rope reins.

Joseph-Armand's garage in Valcourt, 1936

Off they drove down the snow-covered street. Thinking that the machine was far too dangerous, their father ordered them to take it apart. They obeyed.

Joseph-Armand continued his studies for a while, but he was not meant for the priesthood. He was born to be an inventor, and so he left school at 17 to work as an apprentice mechanic in a Montreal garage. Two years later, he was running his own garage back home in Valcourt. But the dream of designing a really good snowmobile stayed with him, and for the next 10 years he experimented with different designs and various sizes of engines.

In 1929 Joseph-Armand Bombardier married Yvonne Lebrecque. Five years later, on a cold winter night, he received a frantic phone call at the garage, where he was working late. Their second son, Yvon,

Joseph-Armand and Yvonne's wedding picture, 1929

was very ill with appendicitis. The doctor told them they must get the boy to the hospital in Sherbrooke, but the heavy snow made the 55-kilometre route impassable. His parents watched helplessly as the little boy died.

This terrible tragedy moved Bombardier to work even harder on his design. A snowmobile would be more than just a means of travel. It could clearly save lives. Then he had a breakthrough. He came up with the idea of a sprocket wheel and track system. He built a machine he named the B-7, which he called the "original work horse." It could carry seven people and was equipped with a heater.

The B-12 model that followed was an immediate success and orders began to pour in. During WWII, Bombardier invented a wide-track armoured troop carrier for the Canadian military that could carry soldiers and equipment across snow. After the war, his wide-track Muskeg tractor became useful for swampy construction work. His business boomed. The machines and the ones that

Bombardier with
the B-7 snowmobile, 1936

Bombardier's armoured snowmobile, 1943

followed were being used all over the world at oil fields, construction sites and lumber camps.

Bombardier never lost his vision of a light machine, something much smaller than the B-12. In 1959 he designed what he called the "Ski-Dog," since he knew all the fur trappers would want one. This manoeuvrable and far less expensive machine became the Ski-Doo.

J. Armand Bombardier in the "Ski-Dog," 1958

Today there are close to four million snowmobilers in North America. Bombardier's company, L'Auto-Neige Bombardier, expanded and began building such machines as aircraft, monorails, high-speed trains and water craft as well as, of course, Ski-Doos. Now Bombardier Inc. has plants all over the world.

A 1960 Ski-Doo sales brochure

A modern Sea-Doo

Joseph-Armand Bombardier became a very successful and wealthy man, but he remained close to his community at Valcourt. He gave the farmers who were employed in his factory time off to work their fields in the summer. He funded an orchestra and sang in the parish choir.

A modern Ski-Doo

Bombardier high-speed train

Today the J. Armand Bombardier Foundation carries on his work, providing grants of money to support charities and education. It also supports the J. Armand Bombardier Museum and the Yvonne L. Bombardier Cultural Centre.

Joseph-Armand Bombardier died on February 18, 1964. Although he was unable to save the life of his son many years ago, his determination to invent the snowmobile has improved travel and communication for people who live in snowy places.

The J. Armand Bombardier Museum

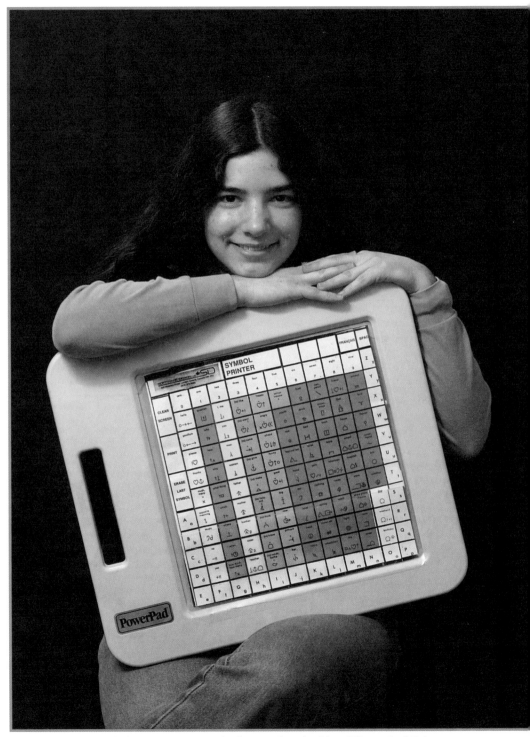

Rachel Zimmerman with the touchpad of her Blissymbol Printer

Rachel Zimmerman

The Inventor of the Blissymbol Printer

On a cloudless night in mid-August 1980, Rachel Zimmerman gazed up at the sky with a sense of wonder. Her parents, Linda and Walter, had driven Rachel and her younger brother, Gary, into the countryside, far from the bright lights of their home on St. James Street in London, Ontario. There, as they did each summer, the family watched the Perseid meteor shower. This year, though, it was more special to Rachel than ever.

She had always liked science, but just months before, Rachel's Grade 2 teacher, Anne Lane, had

Rachel with her horse, Sultan

As a Girl Guide with her brother, Gary

taught her about the planets in the solar system. Her class went on a field trip to the observatory at the University of Western Ontario in London. Looking through a telescope for the first time, Rachel began a relationship with outer space and inventing.

She didn't consider herself to be an inventor in the beginning. A good student, she entered the

OBSERVATORY

The Hume Cronyn Observatory,
University of Western Ontario, London

science fair at St. George's Public School each year with projects including "The Constellation Orion." One of her home inventions had a very practical side. "I invented something I called the 'Great Cake Grate,' which was used to make sure every slice of cake was the same size," she recalls. "This solved the problem of arguing with my brother over who got the biggest piece of cake for dessert."

During Grade 6, 11-year-old Rachel began working on an invention that would end up being useful for people everywhere. She had started reading books about disabilities, and the work of Charles Bliss gave her the idea for her next science fair project. Bliss had invented a universal language called Blissymbolics. In 1972, the year Rachel was born, it was being used enthusiastically by a young teacher at the Ontario Crippled Children's Centre (now Bloorview Macmillan Children's Centre) in Toronto. The language is a system of symbols that can be used by people who have cerebral palsy, who often can neither speak nor control their hand movements well. Wanting to share what she had learned, Rachel Zimmerman did that year's project on Blissymbolics.

Bliss's system of communicating by pointing to symbols was good, but not perfect. By Grade 7 Rachel was working on a computer-controlled device that would let people use Blissymbolics to

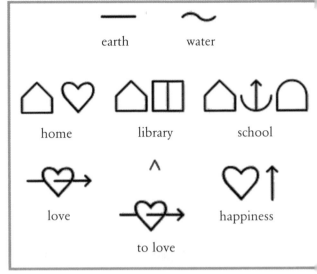

Rachel with her project board at the
Canada-Wide Science Fair in 1985

A few examples of Blissymbols

write messages independently. Her mother, Linda, had a computer software development company. She taught Rachel how to program her computer. Both of her parents greatly encouraged her. So did her Grade 7 teacher, Bill White, with his "Go for it!" attitude.

Rachel created an overlay with 100 Blissymbols and four control keys: new message, backspace, English/French, and print. The overlay was mounted on a touch-sensitive board that plugged into a computer. She then wrote a computer program to make the computer "recognize" the board's symbols. When the user touched a symbol, the computer translated it into a word. Sentences could be seen on the monitor and "typed" on a printer.

Rachel's project placed first in her school science fair. The family went out to her favourite restaurant to celebrate. Her project then won the London and District Science and Technology Fair. The next month, Rachel and her project won a silver medal and an IBM award at the Canada-Wide Science Fair. At 13, Rachel Zimmerman was invited to represent Canada with her project at the World Exhibition of Achievements of Young Inventors in Plovdiv, Bulgaria. She can still remember trying to find Bulgaria on a globe with her brother.

When Rachel was testing the Blissymbol Printer prototype, one boy named Colin used it to tell her how excited he was to have the lead role in his class

With the trophy she won (bottom shelf) for best project at the London District Science and Technology Fair

Rachel displays her project at the World Exhibition of Achievements of Young Inventors in Plovdiv, Bulgaria, 1985

The Women Inventors Project

At the Canadian Space Agency beside
a poster of Canadian astronaut Marc Garneau

play, *The Frog Prince*. To thank him for participating in the prototype test, Rachel embroidered "Prince Colin" on a yellow felt crown and sewed it to a stuffed toy frog, along with a thank-you note written in Blissymbols.

Rachel tested the printer with another Bliss user, Kari Harrington. Kari shared a poem she had written about how she wanted people to see her for who she was inside and not to judge her by her disability. Kari now edits a website for Bliss users.

Rachel Zimmerman went on to London Central Secondary School, then to Brandeis University in the United States and the International Space University

Rachel Zimmerman today

in France. She has worked for the Canadian Space Agency, NASA and other space organizations. Today she is an Education and Outreach Coordinator at Caltech in California, a job that combines her love of science and her commitment to young people and learning. In 2002 Rachel Zimmerman married Scott Brachman, a high school Spanish teacher from Los Angeles.

"Science and engineering are very important to Canada's future," she has said. "Everyone starts out as a scientist, asking questions and exploring the world around them. This natural curiosity can lead to exciting discoveries and new inventions. Never lose your sense of wonder about the world."

Look where that sense of wonder has taken Rachel Zimmerman.

Mike Lazaridis

The BlackBerry Inventor

Mike Lazaridis's mind has always been in motion. Born in Istanbul, Turkey, in 1961, he began thinking along inventive lines from an early age, always wanting to know how things worked. He built a phonograph out of Lego when he was four years old.

With his Greek parents, five-year-old Mike emigrated to Canada from their home in Turkey. The family carried only three suitcases. He can remember flying a bird-shaped kite from the stern of the ship on which they were crossing the Atlantic, fascinated by the way the motion of the vessel and the wind kept the kite in the air.

The Lazaridis family arrived in Montreal, Quebec, and then settled in Windsor, Ontario. Mike's father Nick, who had been a clothing salesman back in Turkey, got a job at the Chrysler factory. His mother Dorothy worked as a seamstress.

Young Mike's scientific mind lit up at the gift of an electric train. He was always tinkering, trying to understand how radios, computers and stereos operated. By Grade 6, his closest friend was Doug Fregin. With another boy, Ken Wood, they spent hours in the Lazaridis basement inventing things.

Ken's mother was a science teacher, and the boys managed to convince her to supply them with chemicals for their experiments. They built working rockets and radios. They used electronic devices to blow up the iodine bombs they made.

One Halloween the boys designed a haunted house. It had a mechanical hand that came clawing up out of the ground. Heads screamed and shrieked, and bats swooped down on the trick-or-treaters.

Mike wanted to go to university, so in high school he took the courses necessary to get him there. But he also took shop courses that let him tinker. Mike and Doug's electronics shop teacher, John Micsinszki, would let them stay after school or come in during the summer and work on their inventions. The two boys entered the high school science fair. Their project, a solar-powered water heater that could track the sun, won the city-wide Windsor Science Fair.

Mr. Micsinszki ran a local ham radio and television club. He told Mike, "Don't get too captivated by computers. In the future, the people who put computers and wireless technology together are really going to come up with something."

After graduating from high school, Mike Lazaridis attended the University of Waterloo, intending to graduate with a degree in electrical engineering. He had earned the money to pay for

The Faculty of Engineering, University of Waterloo

his first year with one of his inventions. It was a buzzer system for his school team that soon had other high schools calling with orders.

In his fourth year he left university with only a month left before graduation. "I did not drop out," he has since said. "I just never finished." He had signed a $600,000 contract with General Motors to design a display board that workers in a noisy factory could look up at to read messages. Mike, working with his old friend Doug, started a company and called it Research In Motion, or RIM.

Years later, in 1997, Lazaridis was working in his basement late at night. He asked himself, "When is a tiny keyboard more efficient than a big one? When you use your thumbs."

That was the beginning of the invention that is now called BlackBerry. It is a wireless device that fits

in the palm of your hand. With it you can make telephone calls, send and receive e-mails, browse the Internet and organize your plans and calendar. The screen takes up about two-thirds of its face. The rest is a keyboard of tiny oval keys that you press with your thumbs. Included are shortcut keys to make working easier.

The difference between BlackBerry and other data devices is that it is always connected. It was with their BlackBerrys that people trapped inside the collapsing World Trade Center towers on September 11, 2001, were able to send out their last messages to family members who would never see them again.

Research In Motion's amazing little BlackBerry has been a brilliant success. In 2000, at the age of 39, president Mike Lazaridis founded the Perimeter Institute with a gift of $100 million. Here scientists

Lazaridis founding the Perimeter Institute in 2000
and receiving the Manning Award in 2002

carry out research in physics.

Science and young people remain very important to Lazaridis. In 2002 when he won the Manning Award, which recognizes Canadian innovators, he used the money to buy new science and engineering books for the libraries in Windsor, where he had grown up. He believes that "there is simply nothing more important we can do than invest generously in science and education."

Today Mike Lazaridis lives with his family in Waterloo, Ontario. There he continues to work at Research In Motion, and to make breakthroughs in a changing world. "In the end," Lazaridis has said, "Nothing replaces hard work."